at that point in time . . .

Claire Léonard

Yvette Contempré

A Sunday afternoon on the great island of Jatte

Text by Yvette Contempré

DUCULOT

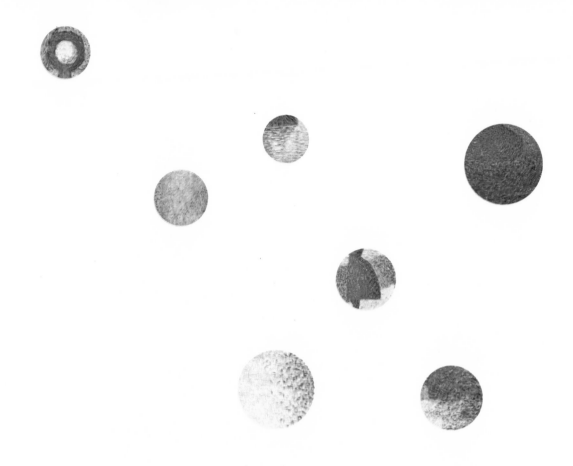

"Oh!" said the little girl, "Please, Ma'am,
give me the colors of the rainbow. I'll
gather them in my apron. I'll make bubbles
and save them in my notebook."

CONVERSATION

"Dearest, I love this spot at sunrise—but look! The shadows grow longer and the afternoon hours steal away. Sadly, I must depart."

"Dear One, I have never doubted the fact that we share so many feelings and common interests. Let us say farewell. I cannot feel sad when we part because I know we shall find ourselves together again soon."

"My walking stick and my hat
give me a look of dignity. But
I happily give up my dignity
on this fading summer afternoon."

"My thoughts are ringed with
circles of smoke. How delicious
to forget all activity on a
fading summer afternoon."

"A stitch knotted, a stitch dropped,
a stitch up over. I embroider the
hours of a fading summer afternoon."

"At Asnières I boarded the
double-decker train. It is
Sunday, a holiday. The Seine
at Courbevoie is really something
to see! At the edge of the great
island of Jatte I hired a boat.
It cost almost nothing.

"I rowed all day long.
The sun bounces off the parasols.
There is a concert, then a dance
tonight. Snow-capped drinks, and dancing
beneath the fragrant bower. Off with
the straw hats, caps and bustles!
Happy day, jolly Sunday, lost in summer's
brilliant light."

"The line.
Will it ever take the line?
Yes, that is the question,"
says the woman fishing. "I have
been waiting long hours for this
wandering trout."

"Mama, do the little boats sailing on the water have legs?" "Of course, my little one, you can see them running in the distance. The pretty woman with the white parasol sings for the rowers who carry her down the Seine."

"I love you, a little, very much, tenderly.
Birds of a feather flock together.
I love you, a little, very much, in spite
of everything.
Hair loose, parasols thrown aside.
I hear the couples whisper, the lapping of
the water, the shouting of the rowers.
I love you, a little, very much—
for an hour."

I love you a little,
.... very much,
tenderly ....

In my very best writing I talk
to you in clever, witty words:
  From sun to shadow
  And shade to sun,
  I jump and leap,
  And leap and run.
  In my lively hopscotch game
  I count parasols, days, and hours.
  I hop towards paradise and
  Add up the colors of the flowers.

"Enormous shadows, organ music
at sunset. I shall tell you
stories that are a little sad.
They shall frighten us a bit,
and make us wonder.
The wolf in the fable is in the woods.
Nearby, the crow has caught something.
The wolf demands that the crow give
it up to him. But this particular
crow, little girl, I know him well!
He cries, 'Caw, caw, caw!' and flies
away laughing. He is the winner."

"Ma'am," says the little girl, "the bubbles flew away. I closed my notebook and summer has gone. I would so like to see the party continue.
"Ma'am," says the little girl,
"I do not want to see the party end."

"Little girl, my little one, step by step we walk on this island. It is dressed in its Sunday best. I gather rainbow-colored bubbles for you. Open your apron now, please don't cry. Little elf, little girl, my little one. Next Sunday the party will begin again on the great island of Jatte. I promise you, we will dance again."

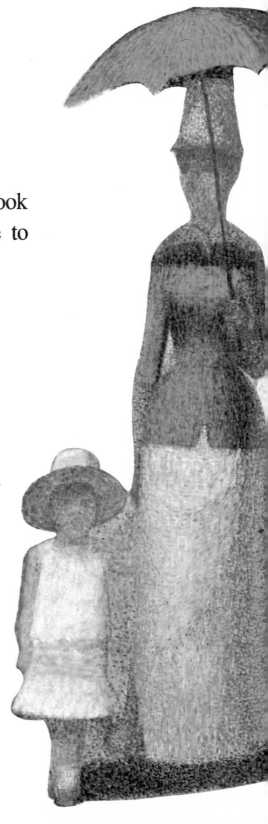

Georges Seurat, 1859-1891

Seurat was a master of "Pointillism," an art form in which small colored dots are arranged side by side. When viewed from the right distance, the dots blend together to form whole images.

Seurat went a step beyond "Impressionism," the popular form of that time. During his short, stubborn, and lonely life, he established a basis for another style of contemporary painting.

There is little doubt that photography helped Seurat develop his new visual form, as shown in his many charcoal drawings.

Jatte is an island in the Seine River in France. Every Sunday, nearly all of Paris gathered at this folksy, happy meeting place, with its cafés, boat races, dances, children's games, and strolling couples. Its lively activity attracted all the innovative painters.

Seurat gave us a peaceful glimpse of the island in a moment outside of time and space. His focus is on the total design and agreement of forms rather than the actual activities shown.

"A Sunday Afternoon on the Great Island of Jatte," painted in 1884-1886, is a large canvas of 207 × 308 cm (approximately 7 × 10 ft). It is presently on exhibit at the Art Institute of Chicago (U.S.A.)

Adapted and Distributed in the United States by:
Silver Burdett Company
Morristown, New Jersey
1979 Printing
ISBN 0-382-06332-5
Library of Congress
Catalog Card No. 79-65866

a point,
period, that's all.

1 2 3 4 5 6 7 8 9 10—CAD—85 84 83 82 81 80